Solids

Lisa Greathous

Consultant

Scot Oschman, Ph.D.
Palos Verdes Peninsula Unified School District
Rancho Palos Verdes, California

Publishing Credits

Dona Herweck Rice, *Editor-in-Chief*; Lee Aucoin, *Creative Director*; Don Tran, *Print Production Manager;* Timothy J. Bradley, *Illustration Manager*; Chris McIntyre, *Editorial Director*; James Anderson, *Associate Editor*; Jamey Acosta, *Associate Editor*; Jane Gould, *Editor*; Peter Balaskas, *Editorial Administrator*; Neri Garcia, *Senior Designer*; Stephanie Reid, *Photo Editor*; Rachelle Cracchiolo, M.S.Ed., *Publisher*

Image Credits

cover FreshPaint/Shutterstock; p.1 FreshPaint/Shutterstock; p.4 (left) Matthew Cole/Shutterstock, (right) Losevsky Pavel/Shutterstock; p.5 Wendy Shiao/istockphoto; p.6 Tom Young/istock; p.7 (top) MarFot/Shutterstock, (left) Gjermund Alsos/Shutterstock, (right) aida ricciardiello/Shutterstock; p.8 (left) Andresr/Shutterstock, (right) Jacqueline Abromeit/Shutterstock; p.9 Maksym Gorpenyuk/Shutterstock; p.10 (top) Lawrence Roberg/Shutterstock, (bottom) Timo Kohlbacher/Shutterstock; p.11 (top) debr22pics/Shutterstock, (bottom) STILLFX/Shutterstock; p.12 Mario Lopes/Shutterstock; p.13 FreshPaint/Shutterstock; p.14 Vulkanette/Shutterstock; p.15 Monkey Business Images/Shutterstock; p.16 Darren Baker/Shutterstock; p.17 xj/Shutterstock; p.18 Smoki/Shutterstock, p.19 Aida Ricciardiello/Shutterstock; p.20 sjeacle/Shutterstock; p.21 (left) evan66/Shutterstock, (center) Bonita R. Cheshier/Shutterstock, (right) Yellowj/Shutterstock; p.22 Michael William/Shutterstock; p.23 Stephanie Reid; p.24 Julija Sapic/Shutterstock; p.25 A. L. Spangler/Shutterstock; p.26-27 Daniela Andreea Spyropoulos/istock p.28 Rocket400 Studio; p.29 Ana Clark; p.32 JoBea Holt

Teacher Created Materials
5301 Oceanus Drive
Huntington Beach, CA 92649-1030
http://www.tcmpub.com

ISBN 978-1-4333-1418-6

Table of Contents

All Around Us

Look around you. What do you see? A window? The book you are reading? A chair? It is all **matter**! Matter is the stuff all around us.

These are all solids.

There are three main kinds of matter: solids, liquids, and gases. Just about everything in the world is one of these.

What Is the Matter?

Which kind of matter do you think this book is? Well, if it were a liquid, it would be dripping off your desk! If it were a gas, it would be floating away in the air. That must make this book a solid!

The air in the balloon is a gas.

The water in the glass is a liquid.

The box is a solid.

One thing all kinds of matter have in common: they all take up space.

A solid is a kind of matter that keeps its own shape. That means that this book will always look like a book. A chair will always look like a chair.

All of these things are solids.

It is hard to change a solid's shape or size. Most solids will not melt if they get hot, and they will not float away!

A solid can be metal, wood, or glass. It can be paper, plastic, or cloth. It can be any color. It can be light as a feather or as heavy as a truck.

These are called **properties**. A property is how an object looks, feels, or acts.

Something in one of these pictures is not a solid. Do you see what it is?

Solids are almost always hard. That is because their **particles** [PAR-ti-kuhls], or parts, are packed tight.

The closer the particles, the harder the solid. A rock has really tight particles!

Tough and Beautiful

Diamonds are one of the hardest natural solids. They can cut glass and steel.

Solids Can Change

Most of the time, matter stays the same. A solid stays a solid. A liquid stays a liquid. But some matter can change if it gets hot or cold.

Liquid Rock

When a volcano erupts, hot lava flows from it. That is just rock that got red hot and turned to liquid!

Can you think of something that can change from a solid to a liquid? How about ice cream left out in the sun?

Even when that ice cream melts, it still tastes the same, right? That is because it is still made out of the same particles.

When the ice cream heats up, its particles get moving. They spread out. That is what makes a solid turn into a liquid.

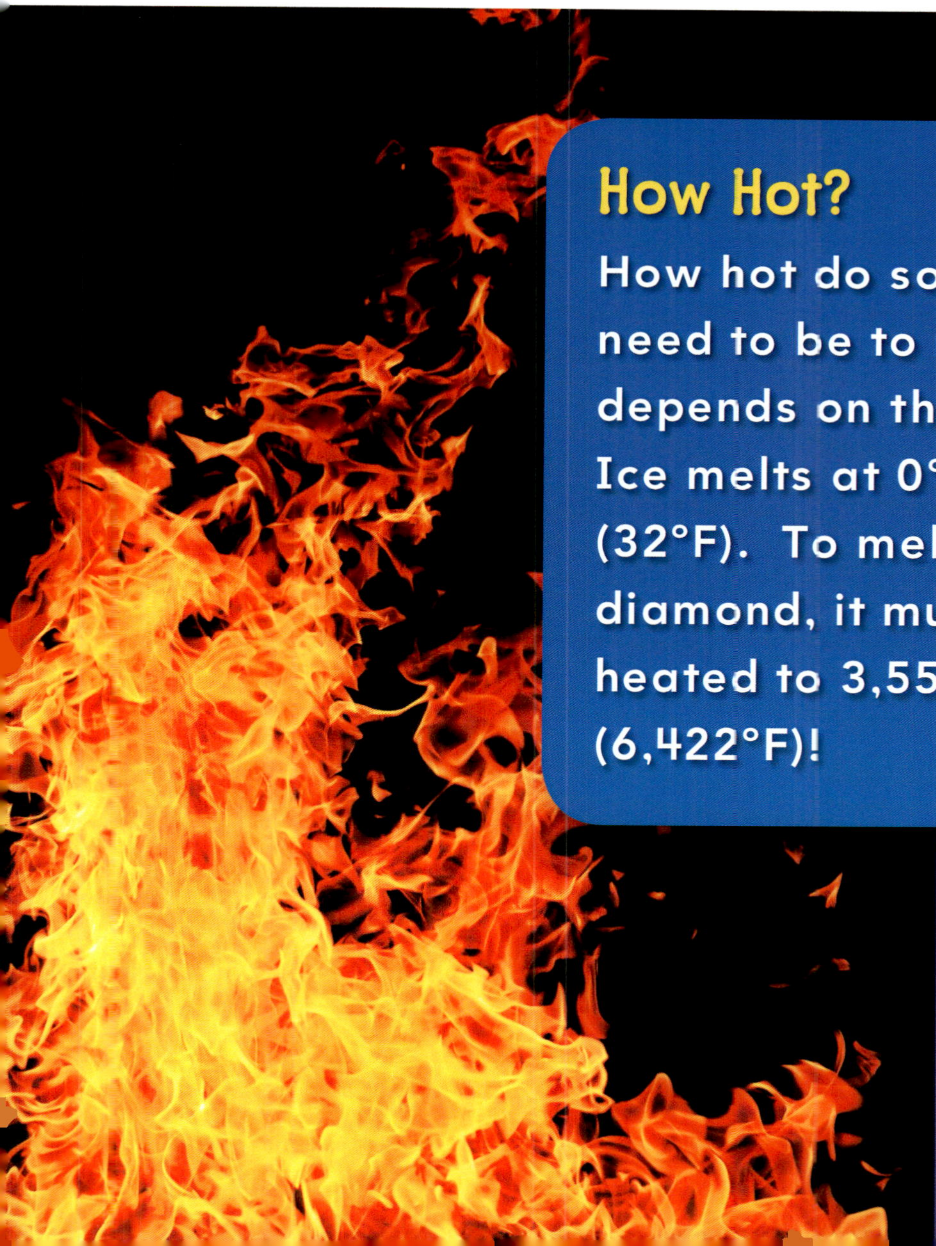

How Hot?

How hot do solids need to be to melt? It depends on the solid. Ice melts at 0°C (32°F). To melt a diamond, it must be heated to 3,550°C (6,422°F)!

A solid's properties change when it turns into a liquid. Unlike solids, liquids can change their shape. Pour water into a tall, skinny glass. The water is tall and skinny.

Pour the same water into a short, wide glass. The water becomes short and wide. That is because a liquid takes the shape of its container.

Liquids can change, too. When a liquid gets hot, its particles start moving fast. They spread out even more.

That can make the liquid turn into gas. That is why you see **steam** coming out of a pot of boiling water.

Water Is Every Kind of Matter!

Sure, water is a liquid. But it turns into a solid when it freezes (like ice or snow). And it turns into a gas when it gets really hot (like steam).

Can you think of a kind of matter that you can not see at all? You are breathing matter right now! The air around you is matter. It is a gas. The particles in a gas are really spread out. They are moving nonstop.

The particles in solids, liquids, and gases move at different speeds.

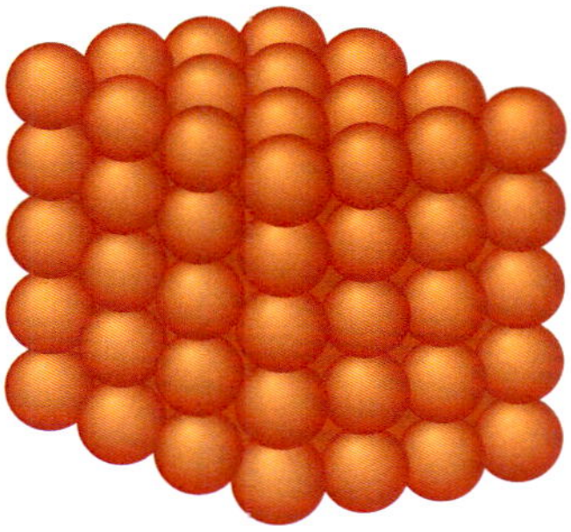

The particles in solids are close together. They do not move at all.

The particles in liquids are farther apart. They slide around each other.

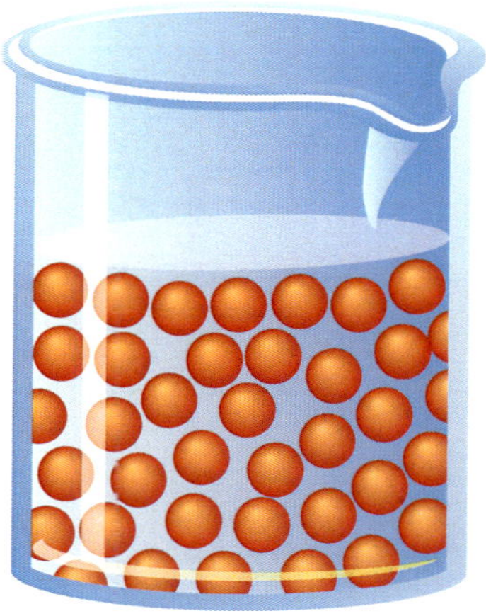

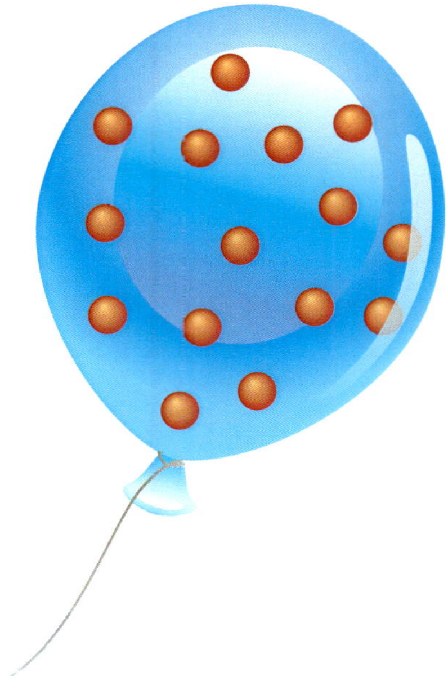

The particles in gases are spread out. They bounce all over!

Think of a bowl of noodle soup. It seems like a liquid, right? But the noodles are solids. And it is so hot, there is steam floating out of it.

That means there are solids, liquids, and gas in that bowl! That is called a **mixture**.

You Matter!

Guess what? You are matter, too! You might think you are a solid. Your bones are solid. But your blood is a liquid.

And you breathe gases in and out of your body, too. That means you are actually a mixture of all three!

Science Lab: Frozen Juice Pops

Turn a solid into a liquid, and then back into a solid that is good to eat!

Materials:

- can of frozen orange juice concentrate
- pitcher to hold juice
- water
- large mixing spoon
- small paper cups
- wooden craft sticks
- freezer

Procedure:

1. Open the can of frozen orange juice and spoon it into the pitcher.
2. Add water according to package directions and mix to make the juice.

3. Fill paper cups about two-thirds of the way with juice.
4. Put the cups in the freezer for one hour.
5. Remove the cups from the freezer and insert the wooden sticks.
6. Return the cups to the freezer for five hours or overnight.
7. Remove the pops from the freezer, peel off the paper cups, and enjoy!

Glossary

matter—anything that takes up space

mixture—blend of two of more different things

particles—tiny parts of something

properties—the ways that an object looks, feels, or acts

steam—gas that comes out of boiling water

Index

A Scientist Today

JoBea Holt is a scientist who put cameras on the Space Shuttle. Students could control the cameras from their classrooms. JoBea thinks students can design great experiments! Now she teaches students about our climate and how it is changing.